LNER LINES
IN THE
YORKSHIRE
RIDINGS

C000157042

by
Peter Cookson & John E.Farline

ACKNOWLEDGEMENTS

Throughout the time during which this book has been compiled we have been very much aware of the debt of gratitude we owe to many people who have made a contribution in one way or another, both large and small. We mention here, by name, John Bateman of Leeds who made the whole of his collection of pictures available to us and helped with a number of matters of identification. Also we mention Bill Hudson who made a considerable contribution in various ways but, particularly, in the area of identification of rolling stock; the detail involved in some of the captions we owe directly to him.

Many other photographers have also been generous with their pictures and, where known, their names have been acknowledged; however, inevitably, there are some pictures that are anonymous but we express here our sincere thanks to all these photographers, known and unknown, whose work we have used. In the case of anonymous pictures the captions represent a best guess on our part and we have tried to make this clear in relevant cases.

Finally we place on record our indebtedness to the Railway Correspondence & Travel Society by virtue of our frequent resort to their monumental work *Locomotives of the* LNER and also, where appropriate, to Willie Yeadon's *Register of* LNER *Locomotives*. When the latter is complete, the two series of books will certainly be indispensable works of reference to all who embark on any book relating to LNER locomotives and their work.

P.C. & J.E.F.

CHALLENGER
PUBLICATIONS

Copyright Challenger Publications, P.Cookson & J.E.Farline 1995
ISBN 1-899624-06-6
Printed and bound by Amadeus Press Ltd, Huddersfield
First published in the UK by Challenger Publications
15 Lovers Lane, Grasscroft, Oldham, OL4 4DP

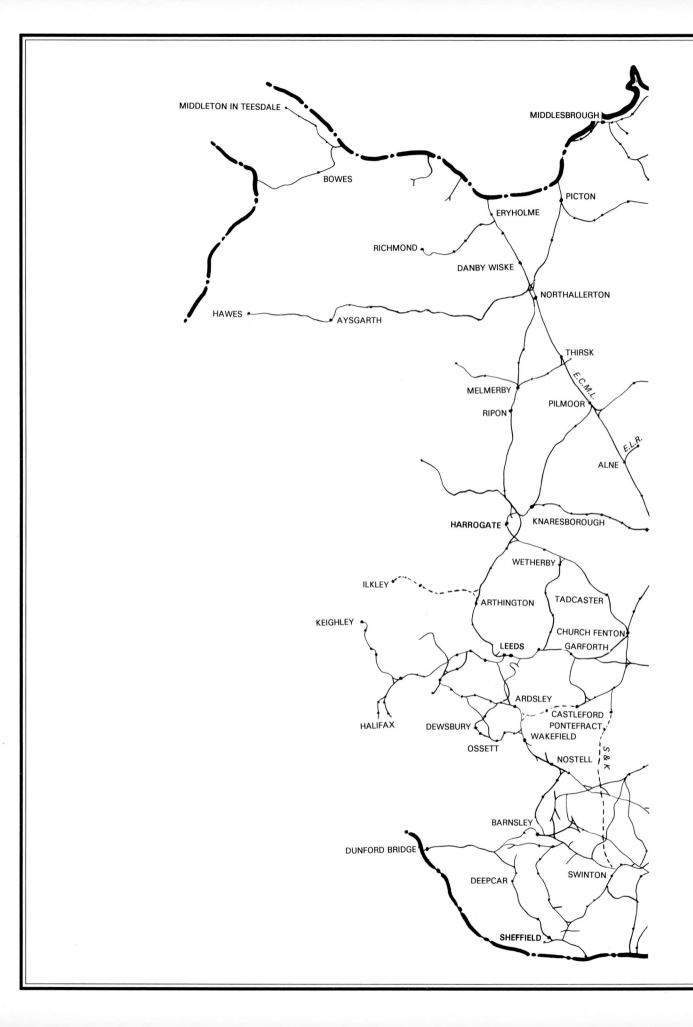

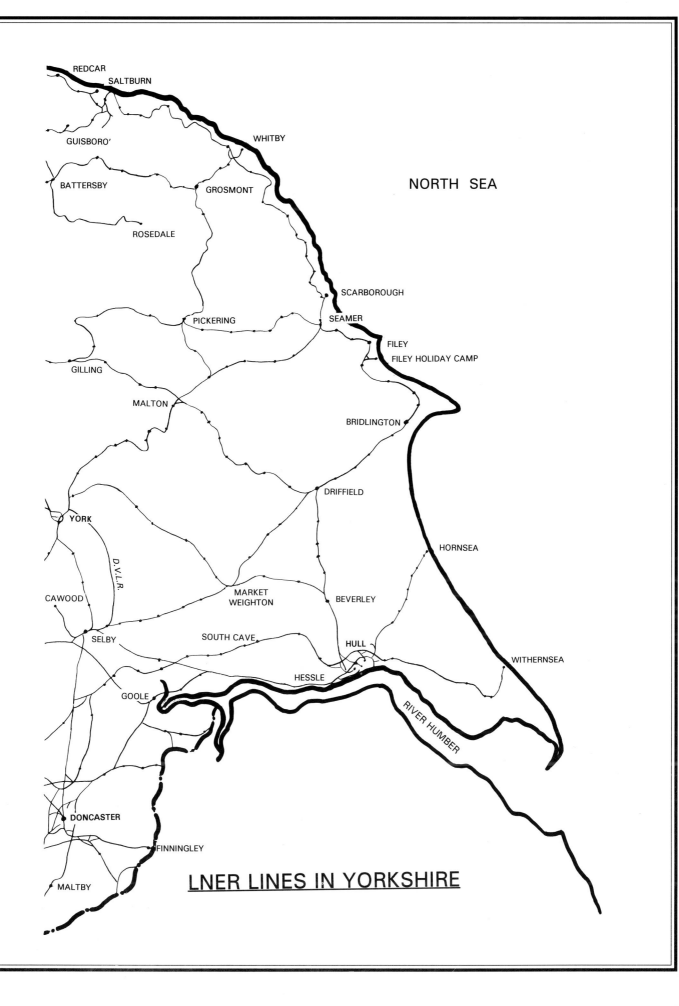

LNER LINES IN YORKSHIRE

INTRODUCTION

This book is not intended to be a history of the LNER Company, nor can it be exhaustive in its coverage of LNER lines in England's largest county. We have tried to put together a collection of photographs which show the variety of trains and scenes found on LNER lines before and after nationalisation within the boundaries of the old Ridings; with a smattering of pre-grouping views on the way. These range from industrial scenes to delightful scenic branch lines through the Yorkshire Wolds, Moors and Dales, the latter being unsurpassed by any other lines in the country for their scenic beauty.

The North and East Ridings were monopolised by the North Eastern Railway up to the grouping of 1923 and in some areas, particularly on the secondary and branch lines, right up to the introduction of diesels. The scene was virtually unchanged with NER locomotives, coaches, signals and buildings still in existence. In the West Riding the Great Northern and Great Central Railways predominated; the GNR mainly in the central area around Leeds and Bradford and the GCR to the south around Sheffield. However, even here the NER made incursions into the territory of the opposition with various joint lines and its lines to Leeds from York, Selby and Harrogate.

During the LNER years new designs of locomotives and rolling stock were introduced and these gradually spread throughout the system. One result of this was that pre-grouping express passenger locomotives which had been used on the East Coast Main Line were downgraded to secondary line use. An example of this was the ex-NER Atlantics which worked their final years on the Hull to Scarborough line.

Railway buildings remained generally the same as before 1923 so that to the casual observer nothing on the railways had changed and, as mentioned above, on the minor lines this situation continued well into nationalisation.

The photographs in the following pages have been grouped into four major areas centred on the cities of Leeds, York, Sheffield and Hull. Although we have tried to keep together those photographs which relate to places in a particular Riding, this has not always been possible. Examples of this are the scenes at Seamer Junction and Seamer Station; both locations were in the North Riding but the photographs have been included in the Hull and East Riding section. This is because the trains in both photographs were heading along the line from Seamer Junction to Hull, the bulk of which was in the East Riding.

Similarly, at Malton, the station was in the East Riding but most of the York to Scarborough line was in the North Riding. (The town of Malton was in the North Riding).

Steam power in Yorkshire survived nearly to the end of B.R. steam operations with the last working LNER locomotives being Class B1 4-6-0s. The Yorkshire Ridings disappeared as administrative areas in the boundary changes of 1974 when the pseudo county names of Humberside, Cleveland, West Yorkshire and South Yorkshire were created. Both West and South Yorkshire have since been removed from the administrative map and, as true Yorkshiremen, we look forward to the day when there might once again be three Ridings.

John.E.Farline., Wakefield.   *Peter Cookson., Pontefract.*

Class J26 0-6-0, No.525, comes off the York avoiding line and trundles past Holgate station as it heads towards Leeds and the west. The leading wagon is a five plank 10 ton, and this is followed by two eight plank 20 tonners, two eight plank 17 tonners, and then a mix of 17 and 20 ton vehicles. These types of mineral wagon were one of the trade marks of the North Eastern Railway and by Grouping over 17,000 of the 20 ton capacity had been built. The LNER continued to build wagons to the same design, but with detailed modifications. Being so numerous the wagons were seen far and wide and complete trains of gas coal ran from the Durham coalfield to East Anglia and Lancashire using these wagons. *W.Hudson collection*

Section One. **Leeds & The West Riding**

One could argue that Yorkshire's industrial West Riding had the most complex railway system in Britain, stemming from the physical and economic geography of the region. The former was basically an east facing slope from the Pennine watershed, down through wooded valleys and out onto the plains and marshes to the east. This slope was intersected by the west-east valleys of four major rivers - the Wharfe, Aire, Calder and Don. These rivers, together with innumerable fast flowing tributaries, of soft, lime-free water, provided ideal conditions for the establishment of fulling mills and domestic weaving. Underlying the area were vast deposits of coal and, in places, ironstone. The importance of these elements was dramatically increased in the late eighteenth century, when steam superseded water power and the Industrial Revolution began. Domestic industry moved into mills and factories, creating a demand for better transport facilities, housing and

commercial development. This progress in turn created employment which led to mass migration from the depressed agricultural south and east. Colliery villages and factory towns seemed to merge into one vast urban sprawl, although the rugged terrain and the Yorkshireman's individuality did not allow this process to finalise. It was indeed a region teeming with people and industry, but without a clearly defined regional centre. It was this presence of many towns and the rich rewards to be gained from the diverse industry that attracted the early railway promoters. Once established the companies strove to expand their empires by putting out tentacles in all directions. With ideal conditions the area continued to grow and, although we have said no one place seemed to form the regional centre, one place had a good claim to it - Leeds. It is here that we begin our brief tour of the LNER lines in Yorkshire.

The machinations which led to the opening of Leeds Central station can probably be considered as the most complex in the history of the West Riding railways. While the full story, so far as it is known, is beyond the scope of the present narrative, suffice it to say that the Great Northern Railway originally agreed to become a partner in building the station in 1846, gaining access to Leeds by running powers over the Midland Railway from Methley, obtained in 1847. A temporary terminus was opened at Central in September 1848, but such were the problems and disagreements that by 1850 there was a general exodus of the companies involved and in that year the GN opened a temporary terminus at low level, access to which involved reversal of all trains at Wortley Junction. The following year the London & North Western, Lancashire & Yorkshire and the Leeds & Thirsk railways agreed to become joint owners of and complete the construction of Central station. In 1854 the GN agreed to become a fourth partner, but it was not until 1857 that the station was completed. In November of that year the company began direct services into Central over the newly opened Bradford, Wakefield & Leeds Railway, and gave up its dependence on the MR for access. From that date the company and its successors were to run its principle services from London Kings Cross into the station for almost 110 years until it was closed on 1st May 1967, after all services had become concentrated on Leeds City station. Throughout this time Central was host to the prestige locomotives of the day, and in this view A4 Pacific 60008 DWIGHT D. EISENHOWER passes Leeds Central 'B' signal box with an up express in the mid 1950s. The Pacific was introduced in September 1937, as 4496 GOLDEN SHUTTLE, it was renamed on 25th September 1945, and received its BR number, 60008, in late October 1948. When photographed it still had its single chimney, but it was fitted with a double one during a casual heavy repair in September/October 1959. Unlike many of its sisters it did not face the cutter's torch and is today preserved at the Green Bay museum, Wisconsin, U.S.A. *C.Marsh*

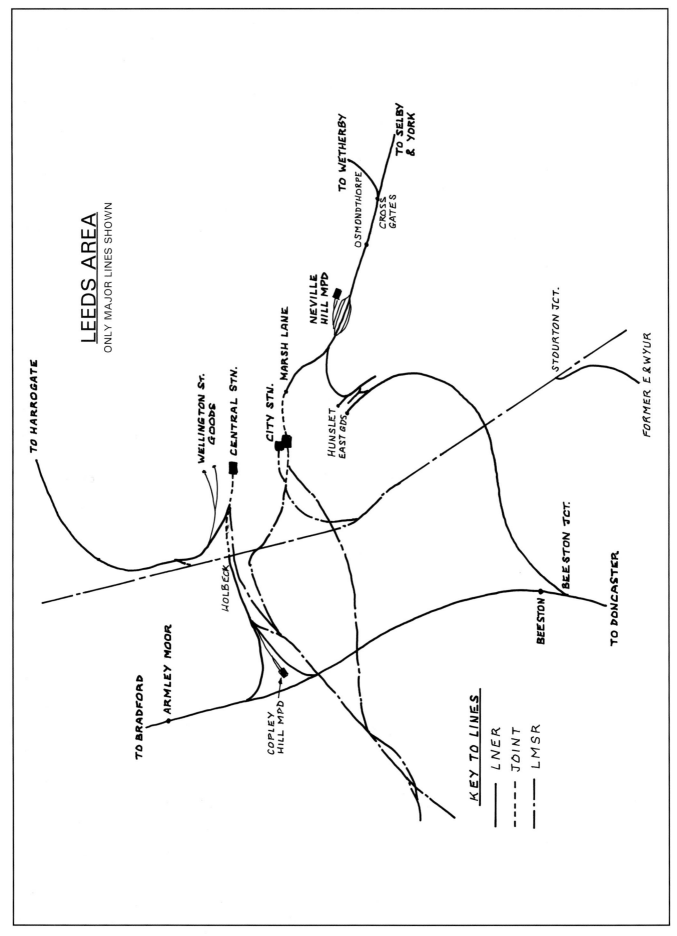

LEEDS AREA
ONLY MAJOR LINES SHOWN

TO HARROGATE

TO BRADFORD

ARMLEY MOOR

WELLINGTON ST. GOODS

CENTRAL STN.

HOLBECK

COPLEY HILL MPD

CITY STN.

MARSH LANE

NEVILLE HILL MPD

HUNSLET EAST GDS

OSMONDTHORPE

TO WETHERBY

CROSS GATES

TO SELBY & YORK

STOURTON JCT.

FORMER E & W YUR

BEESTON

BEESTON JCT.

TO DONCASTER

KEY TO LINES

LNER
JOINT
LMSR

The spartan interior of Central station is seen here as one of the Copley Hill pilots, class J50 No.68988 removes two Pullman cars from the main arrival platform. These vehicles are, in fact, the Leeds portion of the down 'Queen of Scots' Pullman and are being removed for servicing and stabling in readiness for the next day's service. The introduction of Pullman services between London and Yorkshire had its origins on the Great Eastern Railway, which acquired an American General Manager, Mr - later Sir - Henry Thornton, in 1914. With much experience of Pullman travel Thornton saw no reason why Pullman services, then in use south of the Thames, should not prove popular in East Anglia. Accordingly an agreement was drawn up with the Pullman Car Company and various services began. While those on the Continental boat trains from Liverpool Street to Parkeston Quay became very popular, the remainder did not. When the LNER came into being in 1923 there was still a long period of the Pullman Car agreement to run and urgent consideration was given to finding a more profitable use for these vehicles. Apart from the Boat trains the remaining services were withdrawn and a set was made up to run between Kings Cross, Leeds, Harrogate and Newcastle, with the name 'Harrogate Pullman'. In 1925 the service was extended to Edinburgh and later the same year it was re-routed to run non-stop to Harrogate via Shaftholme Junction, Knottingley, Church Fenton and Tadcaster. This change preceded the introduction of a new train, the 'West Riding Pullman' (see page 12). There matters continued until 1928 when a new all-steel set of seven coaches appeared on the service, with the title 'Queen of Scots'. On the same date the 'West Riding' was moved to an afternoon departure from Kings Cross, and the 'Queen of Scots' returned to the Leeds route, leaving London at 11.15am. At the same time it was extended to Glasgow. Little further change took place, until withdrawal during the war, after which its popularity grew, such that by 1952-53 it had grown to a ten-car formation. The down train had a 3 hours 30 minutes schedule to Leeds, where eight of the cars were uncoupled and sent on to Glasgow. During the Beeching regime, when economies were the golden rule the service was curtailed at Harrogate, thus allowing one set of cars to make the return journey daily. As Scotland was no longer being served the title 'Queen of Scots' was dropped, and that of the White Rose' was transferred from its previous owner to the Pullman train. This was short lived however, for with the introduction in 1967 of high speed 'Deltic' hauled eight-coach trains the Pullman service was abandoned. D.Pickersgill Collection

The most likely motive power to be found on local services from Leeds (Central). This is N1 No.69485 polluting its dreary surroundings on the 26th September 1953 whilst awaiting its signal. R.Copeman.

Leeds Central in 1947 with the 'Yorkshire Pullman' departing for the capital behind A3 No.104 SOLARIO. The crew of B1 No.1196 take an interest in the proceedings whilst topping up their charge from the water crane. *W.B.Yeadon collection.*

While we have looked at the GNR services from Central station it must, of course, be remembered that the NER had a very strong presence in Leeds, with services north to Harrogate and eastwards to Hull, York, Scarborough and Newcastle. Originally a somewhat spasmodic service to the east ran from the Midland Railway's Wellington station via Methley, but increasing congestion at the former finally led the NER to deposit Bills, in 1864, for a direct line from Marsh Lane through the city centre to a new station north of Wellington Street. This would have involved such massive destruction of property that local opposition forced the company to abandon the proposal. A revised scheme, on a more southerly route, through some of the worst slums in Leeds, and through the graveyard of St.Peters church, was put forward the following year. (The line was to connect with a new station, to be built jointly by the LNWR and NER, on the south side of Wellington, and subject to rigorous conditions to prevent sacreligious noise and allow the reverent treatment of bodies, the line was approved.) The whole development was completed in 1869 when all LNWR and NER services were transferred to Leeds New station, leaving Central station to the GN and L&Y (although the LNWR continued to run one train annually into the station to preserve its share in the original agreement). Over the years the need for a single station in Leeds was raised from time to time, but it was not until 2nd May 1938 that Wellington and New stations were inter-connected and renamed Leeds City. Further pressure was applied but it was not until after nationalisation that a single passenger station was seen as an economic necessity. A £4.5 million scheme to concentrate all services on City station was put in hand in 1959, but was stopped in 1961 by a curtailment on capital expenditure. The scheme, now reduced in scope, was re-started in 1963. The work included major alteration of the track layout at Copley Hill junction so that traffic on the ex-GN route could gain access to City station. The work also involved the conversion of the former Wellington station into a parcels depot. The expanded City station and the new track layout was brought into use on 1st May 1967, on which day Central station was closed. Although Thomas Prosser's 'New' station had practically no frontage and added nothing to the architectural value of Leeds it did have a distinctive Mansard roof supported by very light trusses carried on foliated columns. At each end of the station were bay platforms for local trains, with traditional longitudinal canopies. These features are clearly seen in this view of 11th July 1949, as A3 Pacific 60086 GAINSBOROUGH stands at the eastern end of the station with an express for Newcastle. When photographed the engine was in pristine condition, having been in service less than two months since it had emerged from Doncaster works in the new pale blue livery.
D.Wilkinson/W.Hudson   collection

9

Few photographs truly capture the spirit of the steam age railway, but this evocative study of the prototype class G5 0-4-4T No.7240 (NER No.1096), at Leeds City on 20th January 1948, encapsulates the dim, smoky atmosphere of a large city station. The G5 tanks were introduced by Wilson Wordsell in 1894 and served for over 50 years with little alteration. Apart from moving the Westinghouse pump from inside the cab to the front of the left hand tank, the only other significant changes were modifications to the bunker to increase coal capacity. In 1917 a cage, with sloping sides, was fitted over the bunker and the rear spectacle plates were altered in shape. In 1921, three engines Nos.1096, 1884 and 1914 had coal rails fitted to the top of the cage. No.1096, along with 30 or so sister engines, was altered again following the introduction of mechanical coaling facilities, when a sheet iron hopper was fitted to the top of the cage to prevent spillage when being coaled. These engines put in sterling work on local passenger trains in Yorkshire and the North East, 7240 serving BR for nearly 10 years before withdrawal in April 1956. *D.Wilkinson/W.Hudson collection.*

(*opposite*) Holbeck High Level station, seen in the background of this view as class A1 No.60141 ABBOTSFORD accelerates away from Leeds with the up 'Harrogate Sunday Pullman', marked the point where the GNR left the joint lines and assumed its own metals. The low level platforms, situated on the Midland route to Bradford and Skipton, were at right angles to the GNR platforms, and were added in 1862, seven years after the high level lines were constructed. The route out of Central station was quite steep and various catch-points were installed to deal with runaways. An interesting example can be seen on the left, where the blades would de-rail an offending vehicle, but a very long lead out would push them inwards, to prevent breaking through the parapet and crashing to the ground below. At first glance the train appears to be un-named, but a very grubby headboard is carried on the centre lamp iron. *C.Marsh.*

A3 60072 SUNSTAR is shown here during its brief five-month period of service working from Leeds Copley Hill shed in the summer of 1960, although its next move was only a very short one - accross the city to Holbeck. The angle of the sun and the headlamp code suggest the working is a late morning or early afternoon Leeds (Central) - Doncaster stopping train. The location is Holbeck (High Level) and Central terminus can just be seen in the centre background. The lines diverging to the left alongside the fourth coach of the train comprises the NER/GNR branch to Geldard junction. R.*Farrell.*

A1 Pacific No 60123 H.A.IVATT, of Ardsley shed, gets into its stride past Wortley South junction signal box with the up 'Yorkshire Pullman', in the late 1950s. Following the success of the Harrogate all-Pullman service introduced in 1923, the LNER sought to expand its activities in this field and the following year it introduced the 'Sheffield Pullman'. This ran from Kings Cross to Grantham and then via Nottingham Victoria to Sheffield Victoria, but it failed to attract custom. A month later it was re-named the 'Sheffield and Manchester Pullman' and was re-routed via Retford to Sheffield and Manchester Central. This too failed to attract significant patronage and in September 1925, following the revision to the 'Harrogate Pullman', the Sheffield set was used to form a new service to Leeds and Bradford. On arrival at Leeds two cars were detached and sent on to Bradford, while the Leeds portion was worked empty to Harrogate to form the 11.15 am to London, via Leeds, where the Bradford cars were picked up. From 1926 the Bradford portion was detached at Wakefield and its working was extended to Halifax. The arrangements were again altered in 1928. When the 'Queen of Scots' was put back on the Leeds route, the Harrogate set was renamed the 'West Riding Pullman' and its down departure time was changed from 11.10am to 4.45pm, thus giving Yorkshire passengers the benefit of two daily Pullman services. In 1935 it was decided to extend the service to Hull, the relevant portion being attached and detached at Doncaster. In view of this wider range of operation the train was renamed the 'Yorkshire Pullman'. In the autumn of 1937 the introduction of the 'West Riding Limited' streamliner service, with a mid-morning departure from Leeds, negated the need for a morning Pullman service from Bradford and Leeds. The Harrogate train was therefore diverted via York, before calling at Doncaster to pick up the two Hull cars, and the two which had been worked from Halifax via Bradford and Wakefield. Following reinstatement after the war, by which time it had returned to the Leeds route, various departure times were tried until in 1949, the train settled down to a 10.15am departure from Harrogate and a 5.30pm return from Kings Cross. The final changes to the service began with a cut in journey times following the introduction of 'Deltic' diesels, and the concession to Hull of its own Pullman service in 1967, which then allowed the 'Yorkshire Pullman' to run non-stop to Wakefield. The train continued to run until the end of the 1977/78 timetable, on a schedule of 2hr 55 min, but was then quietly forgotten. It has now been re-instated and runs today with Mk.4 coaching stock and electric Class 91 haulage. There are two sets of carriages, and such has been the acceleration of timings, that each set makes two return journeys daily between Leeds and Kings Cross. C.Marsh

Former GC 4-4-2T, LNER class C14, No.7446, heads away from Beeston station into Leeds with a local train from Wakefield or Castleford, just after the war. The train is composed of a single pair of Gresley articulated stock (brake third and lavatory composite), with an eight compartment third at the rear. The C14s spent a long time in the West Riding, No.7446 being shedded at Ardsley when photographed, as clearly shown in traditional LNER style on the buffer beam. The engine was withdrawn at the end of 1956, by which time it had been transferred to Gorton.
P.Cookson collection

Another Leeds area local train of the same period, with ex GN class N1 0-6-2T No.9436, slowing for the Beeston stop with a Leeds - Castleford (Central) working. The train formation is exactly the same as the previous illustration, but the engine is too grubby to ascertain its depot, which would have been either Ardsley or Copley Hill. The N1s, perhaps more than any other type, were the typical motive power for LNER suburban services around Leeds and Bradford, until their withdrawal with the introduction of diesel multiple units in the mid 1950s. *P.Cookson collection*

Gresley A3 No.60052, PRINCE PALATINE, finds itself on a very humble duty working an evening Doncaster-Leeds local past Ardsley motive power depot, in the mid 1950s. It was not unusual to find this kind of working as Pacifics were often rostered for local trains as part of a more complex diagram. In the case of Doncaster-Leeds services they were also used as 'running-in' turns after overhaul at the 'Plant'. The most interesting element of the scene, however, is the train itself. The leading coach is an ex GC matchboard corridor third, in carmine and cream livery, behind which appears to be an ex LNWR brake third. At the rear is an unidentified eight compartment third. *C.Marsh*

The down 'Queen of Scots' Pullman races past Spring Lane, Ardsley with A1 No.60134 FOXHUNTER at the head. Completed in November 1948, this locomotive was withdrawn in October 1965, having spent much of its short working life at Copley Hill depot. The confusing array of signals is not as complex as might at first appear; the original wooden post, with its mixture of upper quadrant and somersault arms, was shortly to be replaced by a fabricated steel structure seen a couple of yards or so in front, but without arms. C.*Marsh*

A class J empty wagon train is seen in the vicinity of Tingley gas works, circa 1957, hauled by an unidentified Class O4 2-8-0 locomotive (probably from Ardsley shed) on the line from Adwalton Junction to Ardsley. The line seen curving in from the left is the branch from Batley (GN) through Woodkirk to Tingley. A.M.*Ross.*

(*above*) Reproduced from a copy of an old postcard, this picture of Stanley station, Methley Joint Railway, looking west towards Lofthouse Junction shows the attractive design of the main station buildings on the left; the steep angles of the hipped roofs are particularly noticeable. *J.E.Farline collection*

(*right*) Stanley signal box, situated on the opposite side of the main Wakefield - Aberford road from the station. Although the Methley Joint Railway involved the GN, NER and L&YR it was the first mentioned that had the principal interest and the stations and works along the line were of GN origin. The decorative barge-boards of the signal box are noteworthy as is the GNR somersault signal to the left with its spectacles about one third of the way down the signal post. *J.E.Farline collection*

A lovely period-piece photographed at Earlsheaton (near Dewsbury) some time before 1914. The locomotive crew and shunting staff pose proudly with their immaculate GNR Class L1 (LNER Class R1) 0-8-2T No.128 during shunting operations. These locomotives were originally a development of Ivatt's 0-8-0 mineral engine and intended for London suburban work but they proved to be too heavy and generally unsuitable, whereupon they were banished to the West Riding and Nottingham districts for freight working. No.128 was an Ardsley engine until it and its sisters were sent to join the others at Colwick early in 1914. J.E.Farline collection.

An unidentified B1 4-6-0 has just passed Earlsheaton station as it hurries a three coach formation of brake first, corridor composite and brake third, from Bradford to Wakefield, where they will be attached to a Leeds - King's Cross express. The original GN line from Wakefield to Bradford ran via Ossett and Batley, but the GN were keen to tap the lucrative traffic from Dewsbury, the centre of the heavy woollen industry. Consequently powers were obtained for a loop line from Runtlings Lane junction, west of Ossett, to serve Dewsbury. This was opened to a temporary station in the town in 1874, but this was a time of industrial depression and it was not until 1880 that a permanent station was opened and the loop to Batley completed. This line then became the principal route from Wakefield to Bradford and remained so until closure in 1965. The line passing through the gate on the extreme left served a colliery. A.M.Ross

Ex GNR 0-6-0 No.64268 (LNER Class J6), of Ardsley shed, approaches Runtlings Lane junction, a little under a mile east of Earlsheaton, with a short coal train in the late 1950s. The train is running from one of the many collieries in the Dewsbury/Batley area to Wrenthorpe yard, Wakefield and is probably returning the two leading brake vans to the yard to await their next turns of duty. The rather dilapidated single branch line climbing away to the right is the original line from Ossett to Batley via Chickenley Heath, opened in 1864; the line via Dewsbury (Central) was opened rather later in 1880 and assumed the greater importance for traffic between Wakefield and Bradford. In terms of physical geography the line abounded in severe gradients and many of the heavier trains - particularly longer excursion trains - had to be double-headed. A.*Robinson*

The Chickenley Heath branch, mentioned in the previous caption, is the setting for 'Ardsley tank', LNER class J50/2, No.68916, with a short mineral train in the early 1950s. The leading 12 ton wooden wagon is a former private owner wagon, still with pre 1923 round bottom grease axleboxes, but though it has traces of its original livery this is sadly indiscernible. The second wagon is also an ex private owner with 'cupboard' style side doors. In later years the branch was largely disused at the Runtlings Lane end but it was in regular use at the Batley end to service Shaw Cross Colliery until that pit closed about 1960. It was normal practice to work coal down to Batley yard in very short trains because of the severe gradients, as typified by this view of 68916 near Shaw Cross. A.M.*Ross*

A Leeds - Doncaster local train rolls into Wakefield Westgate behind class A2/2 No.60505 THANE OF FIFE. The A2/2's were Thompson's rebuild of the Gresley class P2 2-8-2's introduced in 1934 for the arduous Edinburgh - Aberdeen route. At nationalisation all six of the A2/2's were in service in Scotland but came south at the beginning of the 1950s, being equally divided between York and New England sheds. The train consists of a Thompson brake third and matching full third, followed by a Gresley composite and brake third. C.*Marsh*

The down 'Queen of Scots' Pullman comes off the '99 arches' viaduct and through the middle road at Wakefield Westgate behind A1 No.60120 KITTIWAKE, a type which dominated haulage of this train. By the time of this illustration, in the late 1950s, the original GN platform canopies, with their familiar saw-tooth barge boards, had been replaced by the featureless reinforced concrete design then in vogue. Today much of this scene remains, but the overall appearance has been greatly changed by the addition of overhead electrification wires and masts. A.*Robinson*

The Methley Joint line was an undertaking involving the GNR, NER and LYR, although the former had the major interest in it, and made the greatest use of it. The principal use of the system was the movement of coal, but for much of its life it did carry local services from Leeds (Central) and Wakefield (Westgate) to Castleford. It also enabled occasional excursion trains from Rothwell, on the East & West Yorkshire Union Railway, to run via Lofthouse Junction, Methley Joint Junction and Castleford to get to the east coast resorts of Scarborough or Bridlington. In latter years it also provided an ideal line for enthusiasts tours and this view shows one such Railway Correspondence & Travel Society special behind two class J6 0-6-0s. The leading engine, 64222 is from Ardsley shed, which normally provided motive power for workings in the area. E.E.Smith.

O2/4 No.63947 slogs up the slow line at Hemsworth with a train of South Kirkby coal, in an almost equal mix of wooden and all-steel mineral wagons, in September 1958. The three cylinder class O2 2-8-0's were Gresley's ultimate heavy freight locomotives and they saw a great deal of service on loose coupled coal trains such as this one. Visually they were handsome, well proportioned engines, but there was considerable variation within the class, depending on the type of boiler, cab or tender fitted. 63947, with 100A boiler, side-window cab and group standard 4200 gallon tender, makes a pleasant sight in the evening sunshine as she earns her keep in typical fashion. P.Cookson

Excursions to the east coast from points on the GNR system in West Yorkshire, such as Batley, Bradford, Ossett etc., which used the Methley Joint line to avoid Wakefield, were very often double-headed as far as Castleford, where the pilot would be detached. It was usual on summer evenings at weekends to find light engines waiting at Castleford for returning excursions in need of assistance over the heavy gradients on the final part of their journey. Such a sight is typified here with an Ardsley J6, still in LNER livery, and a named B1 in LNER apple green with BR number and lettering, standing on the Cutsyke branch just to the west of Castleford station. D.*Pickersgill collection*

A down Class H freight passes Castleford goods yard between the station and the level crossing signal box on 25th August 1960. The locomotive is Class B16/2 No.61435 - one of Gresley's 1937 rebuilds of the original Raven design. Both Gresley and Thompson produced modifications to the original locomotives, the latter being designated class B16/3. Although the rebuilds were very similar in appearance, they could be readily identified by the fact that the Gresley engines were right-hand drive, while the Thompson machines were left-hand drive. P.*Cookson*

A very grimy class Q6 0-8-0, No.63424, makes heavy weather of lifting a loaded coal train up the grade out of Kippax on the single line branch from Castleford to Garforth, about 1960. The branch was opened in 1878 as the Leeds, Castleford & Pontefract Junction Railway, but was worked from the outset by the NER. In the main it was a freight line, having been built to exploit collieries in the Kippax and Allerton Bywater areas, but until 1951 carried a Leeds City - Castleford local service. In this view the train is moving very slowly as the wind is carrying the smoke ahead of it! M.*Baldwin*

Thirty years ago the annual seaside holiday meant a journey by train for many, if not the majority, of holidaymakers and the next two views show such trains near Pontefract (Baghill) on the Swinton & Knottingley Joint line. With its connections to the Midland at Dearne Junction, the GCR system at Mexborough West Junction and the Barnsley - Manchester line via the Wath curve, the S&K Jt line was well placed to handle the heavy excursion traffic to the east coast via York or via Milford Junction and Selby. In this view a very clean Mexborough K3, 61868, with a train of ex LMS Period II and III stock, is seen just south of Pontefract on 30th August 1958. Although the reporting number is partially obscured by the vacuum hose, the train appears to be the Sheffield Victoria - Filey Holiday Camp train. Not only the use of the LMS stock is of interest, but the fact that four of the vehicles are still in carmine and cream a good two years after the 1956 livery changes. P.*Cookson*

Travelling south, in roughly the same location as the previous view, in the early afternoon is B16/1 No.61419, of Selby shed, with the Scarborough (Londesborough Road) - Leicester (Central) holiday train via the GC line. The hill behind the smoke is Bag Hill, from which the station took its name. The NER slotted past signal on the left is worthy of note. *P.Cookson*

One train which ran for many years over the S&K line and regularly brought Southern Region coaching stock to the north east was the Newcastle - Bournemouth through train, which ran via the GC route, Banbury and Oxford. This train is seen climbing out of the Aire valley, on 1st May 1958, and approaching Pontefract, the first stop from York, behind 61457 one of York's numerous B16/2s. These locomotives were regular performers over the line, on all types of trains from express passenger to local freight. *P.Cookson.*

The return working off the Brackenhill branch on Thursday 22nd May 1958, approaches Pontefract (S&K) from the south conveying coal from Hemsworth Colliery, ultimately, mainly bound for Gascoigne Wood yard, but initially to Pontefract (Baghill) for intermediate sorting. The locomotive (almost invariably at this time) is one of Selby's stud of Q6 0-8-0s no.63432. The Brackenhill branch, although designated a light railway, was in fact, able to take the largest freight locomotives and in its latter days (after the closure of Selby shed) was host to all kinds of freight locomotives - whatever appeared to be on hand at York shed suitable for the job. *P.Cookson*

Recently shopped Mexborough B1 No.61165, restarts a through goods from a temporary stop alongside Burton Salmon station in 1958. The NE splitting signal indicates that the train is bound for Ferrybridge and Pontefract, en route to Mexborough and Sheffield. On the passenger lines, to the left, the NE signals have been replaced by an LNER structure, which when photographed showed the road set for Castleford and Normanton. Both the station and junction have now disappeared from the scene, but four running lines remain and are still heavily used. *P.Cookson*

B1 No.61016 INYALA passes Low Moor No.2 signal box, on the L&Y Bradford (Exchange) - Halifax route, with an express, probably bound for Manchester (Exchange). Seen here, sometime after 1959, when the electrification flashes were added to the running plate, this locomotive led a somewhat nomadic existence during its final years. In 1956 it was shedded at York, but was transferred to Neville Hill in 1957. It stayed there for several years, but had been sent to the ex-L&Y engine shed at Low Moor by 1964, from where it was withdrawn during the last week of October 1965. From behind the signal box in the right background a GNR branch ran to Dudley Hill, off which was a spur to a GNR goods depot situated some distance to the right. Neither of these could have attracted much traffic as they were closed as early as May 1933. *J.Bateman collection*

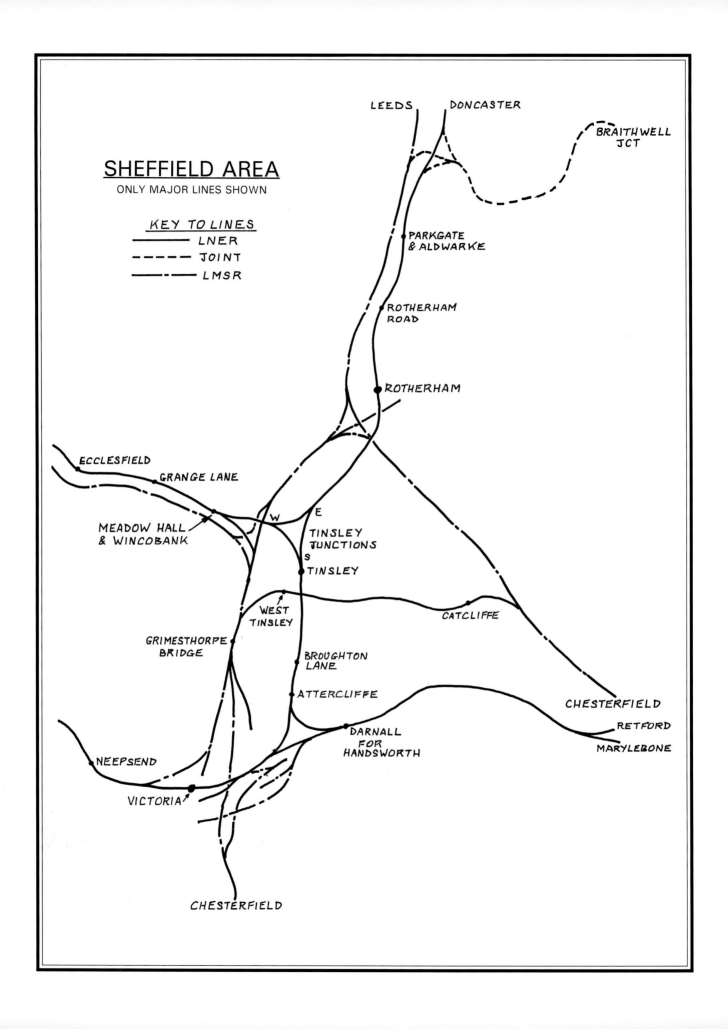

Penistone was effectively a railway crossroads, with ex GCR lines running westwards to Manchester via Woodhead, southwards to Sheffield and east to Barnsley and Doncaster. To the north was the ex LYR line to Denby Dale and Huddersfield, with the main station buildings located in the vee between the Manchester and Huddersfield lines. Penistone, with a population of just over 6,000 was a small, but important manufacturing and market town on the eastern slopes of the Pennines and the terminus of a number of local services. As far as the LNER was concerned stopping trains from Doncaster, Barnsley and Sheffield had Penistone as their destination. These trains were virtually monopolised by ex GC locomotives until withdrawal of services in 1959. Shown here is a typical service with class J11/1 0-6-0 No.64343, of Barnsley shed, leaving Penistone with a local train back to its home town. E.Blakey.

37

38

(*opposite*) Barnsley, like Sheffield and Wakefield, suffered from George Stephenson's policy when building the North Midland Railway, of adhering to maximum gradients at the expense of by-passing important towns. As a result Barnsley's 'main line' station lay 3 miles north east of the town centre, at Cudworth. For thirty years this meant a road journey, but in 1870 a branch was opened from Cudworth South Junction to Barnsley Court House. Although the latter was jointly owned by the MR and MS&LR, it was the Midland and its successors which worked the passenger services to Cudworth, almost up to their withdrawal in June 1958. However, for a short time from 1957, displaced C14 class 4-4-2Ts from Gorton shed were sent to Barnsley to eke out their final days on local trains in that area. One such service was that to Cudworth headed by 67448, with painted 36D on the smokebox door, standing in platform 3 at Cudworth on a dismal day in June 1957. The train consists of a Stanier nine compartment non-corridor third and a six compartment brake. *J.F.Sedgwick*

(*opposite bottom*) During the preparation of the Act for the proposed Midland line from Cudworth to Barnsley it was agreed that the station planned for Barnsley would become the joint property of the MR and the MS&L. Before this the MS&L had used the 'bottom' station, but the general state of the station and the curving, 1 in 50 start on the Penistone line (opened throughout on 1st December 1859) were far from ideal. When the MR line opened in May 1870 a temporary station was brought into use, but during 1871/72 the adjoining Barnsley Court House was adapted to form a station and the name was retained. The station had a lightweight overall roof, with wooden platforms below and timber screen walls either side. The principal services using Court House were all local trains, either Sheffield-Barnsley or Doncaster-Penistone, one of which is seen in the mid 1950s behind class C13 4-4-2T 67434. On the left stands the driving trailer of the Barnsley-Cudworth push-pull unit, the other regular service from the station. *N.E.Stead collection*

(*below*) A superb overall view of Barnsley engine shed and Exchange station, together with Jumble Lane crossing and its associated signal box. The line from the Midland Railway at Wincobank & Meadow Hall to the Manchester and Leeds Railway at Horbury was opened in stages between 1850 and 1854, with the section north of Barnsley opening first. Prior to the opening it had been agreed that the line should be leased to the M&L, while the southern portion was worked, when opened, by the South Yorkshire Railway. This eventually led to the unusual situation of an end-on junction in the centre of the station (which carried the suffix Exchange between 1st August 1924 and the closure of the adjoining MR Court House station in 1960) between the L&Y and GC. The most unusual aspect of Exchange was that it only had one platform, a feature which the authors cannot readily explain. It was almost certainly not a question of lack of space for in the 1850s the town was quite small; nor was it the proximity of the engine shed. The original locomotive facilities consisted of a single road shed north of the station, near Old Mill Lane bridge. The depot seen here was built much later by the GCR, whose locomotive designs always dominated the allocation. Being a freight depot the engines on view are mainly 0-6-0 and 2-8-0 tender types, with three class C13 4-4-2 tank engines, 67447 nearest the camera, used for passenger workings to Penistone, Doncaster and Sheffield. The signal box is so nondescript as to defy classification and may well be the original box built by the South Yorkshire Railway, although the flat roof is a modern feature. Barnsley shed was closed on 4th January 1960 and the site cleared. Opportunity was then taken to add a second platform to the station and a footbridge. *P.Cookson collection*

Space was always a problem at Barnsley, for the land fell away quite steeply just north of the shed, and it was normal practice at weekends to stable locomotives some distance from the shed, south of the Midland route into Court House. Such a scene is depicted on Sunday 19th May 1957, with ex GC 2-8-0s dominant. On the right is class O4/8, No63731, which has obviously been subject to a bit of rough shunting. Part 8 of class O4 was a Thompson rebuild using the chassis of the O4, but incorporating a new standard 100A boiler and a new design of side-window cab. On the left stands 63913 of class O4/6; this engine was one of eleven rebuilt from class O5 in 1924. W.Potter

Like Barnsley, Mexborough engine shed was primarily a freight depot and this 1947 view shows one of the usual inhabitants, ex GC class J11/3 0-6-0, No.4442. This class was a Thompson rebuild of the original Robinson design, using piston valves and incorporating shorter boiler mountings. As such they came to be regarded as a standard class under Thompson's rationalisation of locomotive classes in the early 1940s. Behind 4442 can be seen one of the huge S1/3 0-8-4 tank engines, 9905, used for hump shunting in Wath yard. The original 3-cylinder locomotives had been built by J.G.Robinson in 1907 for this specific duty, but 9905 was rebuilt by Gresley in 1932 with various refinements to the original design including side window cab and sloping side tanks to improve forward vision. At the same time boosters were fitted to the trailing bogie to enhance power on the very arduous task for which they were designed, but the boosters were later removed. *Lance Brown*

A collection of ex-NER 0-6-0 tank engines await their next turn of duty at Alexandra Dock, Hull. This was the site of the Hull & Barnsley two road wooden engine shed built in the 1880s. By 1913 it was decided that it was beyond repair and should be replaced. However, this did not happen and it remained in use until December 1927. Demolition then took place but a replacement shed was never provided with the result that engines had to stand out in the open air. On 27th October 1963, Alexandra Dock's allocation of locomotives was transferred to Dairycoates although the old shed area was retained as a signing-on point. R.J.*Buckley*

Class Y8 0-4-0T Nos.563 and 560 stand inside Hull Dairycoates shed during 1931. This was the largest locomotive depot on the North Eastern Railway and the engines were two of the smallest to work on the LNER. Designed by T.W.Worsdell as NER Class K, they weighed 15½ tons and had a tractive effort of 6,000 lbs. They were introduced in 1890 and the last one was withdrawn in 1956. *Locofotos*.

One of Robinson's "Large Director" 4-4-0s, LNER class D11/1 No.2665 MONS, heads a Hull-Sheffield (Victoria) express near Ferriby in 1947. The locomotive is carrying its 1946 number which it would have borne for only two or three years before renumbering in the British Railways fleet. A.L.Brown

A stopping train for Hull leaves Withernsea behind L1 67754 of Botanic Gardens shed about 1955. Note the unusual design of NER bracket signal on the left. The station layout was also unusual as there was a turntable at the end of the line behind the train. The Hull & Holderness Railway was built as an independent line and was one of the few in the North East which had its own locomotives and coaches. Opened on 28th June 1854, the H&HR worked the line up to the end of 1859 when the NER took over working of the line. Authority for amalgamation was given on 7th July 1862. J.F.Oxley

B1 61377 approaches Wansford Box at the north end of Driffield station on its way to the coast with a trainload of holidaymakers. In the left background is Driffield goods warehouse which was designed by the Y&NMR architect G.T.Andrews. Other Andrews buildings, with their typical wide overhanging eaves, can be seen on the right and behind the coaches at the rear of the train. A.M.Ross.

A year before the final closure of the Malton to Driffield line in 1958, class J27 0-6-0 No.65849 of Malton shed (50F) shunts the twice weekly pick-up goods at Sledmere & Fimber station. The passenger service had been withdrawn in 1950 although it was occasionally re-instated during periods of heavy snow to provide transport for stranded villagers. A.M.Ross

A view at the south east of Sledmere & Fimber station looking towards Malton. J27 No.65849 waits for the manual crossing gates to be opened before proceeding across the B1248 Beverley to Malton road. The sign on the cottage on the left states that this is Fimber Road. As can be seen, the road crossed the railway at a very acute angle with the result that the gates at each side of the crossing were a considerable distance apart. A.M.Ross

A J27 0-6-0 passes the disused chalk quarry at Burdale, between Wharram and Sledmere, just after leaving Burdale tunnel. The tunnel was just under a mile in length. The buildings along the line, including the cottage in the left background, used bricks which had the letters "M & DR" pressed into them. The Malton & Driffield Railway was an independent line which opened on 19th May 1853. It climbed over the Wolds with gradients between 1 in 64 and 1 in 104. A.M.Ross

D49/2 62756 THE BROCKLESBY blasts through Carnaby station just south of Bridlington with a stopping train from Scarborough to Hull during a bright winter's day in the mid 1950s. Gresley's large 4-4-0s, both "Shires" and "Hunts", were the most common engines used on this line after the war up to the introduction of diesel multiple units in the late fifties. 62756 was allocated to Neville Hill shed. A.M.Ross

B16s galore at the southern end of Bridlington station. A B16/1 in the background is obscured by B16/2 No.61421 which is double-heading B16/3 no.61467 on a Bridlington - Castleford return excursion. The load of 12 bogies probably justified the assistant engine for the climb over the Wolds. Designed by Sir Vincent Raven as NER class S3, the B16's were used throughout Yorkshire on all types of traffic from slow goods to express passenger. In 1937, No.2364 was rebuilt by Gresley and incorporated his system of Walschaerts valve gear for the outside cylinders and derived motion for the inside cylinder. Six more engines were also rebuilt and given the classification B16/2. In 1944 further rebuilds were authorised by Thompson but this time with three separate sets of Walschaerts valve gear. Seventeen engines received this treatment and became class B16/3. The train is passing under one of the two magnificent NER signal gantries which were adjacent to Bridlington South signal box; the box is just off the left hand side of the photograph. A.M.Ross

A venerable pair of ex-NER 4-4-0s of class D20, No.62395 and its unidentified sister, leave the south end of Bridlington station with the 11.25 a.m. Scarborough (Londesborough Road) to Liverpool (Exchange)in August 1955. The D20s (LNER classification) were the NER class R, designed by Wilson Worsdell and introduced in August 1899 for use on express passenger trains on the east coast main line north of York. Above the second engine can be seen the extension to the original Y&NMR train shed roof which was built in a different style. On the left the support wall for the coal cells can be seen plus a slotted timber post bracket signal. On the right is an ex-NER gas tank wagon. J.W.Armstrong

All the Big Four railway companies had substantial numbers of the versatile 0-6-0 tender locomotive and, during the 1950s, notwithstanding that most of their work was rather mundane and unglamorous, they were often called on at week-ends to work main-line passenger trains. Helping out with a summer Saturday express passenger working and having already conquered the 3½ miles at 1 in 95/100 from Market Weighton up to Enthorpe, valiant J11 No.64286 faces almost 5 miles of 1 in 92 on leaving Bridlington with the 10.30 a.m. Sheffield (Victoria) - Filey Holiday Camp in late August 1953. A.M.Ross.

Scarborough shed's one and only B16, 61445, climbs the 1 in 92 bank from Bridlington to Speeton just north of Flamborough station with the summer Saturdays only 9.52 a.m. Gloucester to Filey holiday camp. This train ran via the Midland "Old Road" between Tapton Junction and Rotherham Masborough. The B16 had taken over from an LMR engine at Masborough Station South, having worked out there earlier in the day with a Leicester train from Scarborough and then going on shed at Canklow. The section of line from Bridlington to Filey was opened one year after that from Seamer to Filey. The delay was caused by difficulties in cutting through the chalk across Flamborough Head, some of which can be seen in the photograph. The first four coaches of the train are ex-LMS vehicles and comprise: Stanier brake third, Stanier third open, Stanier corridor third and another Stanier design of unidentifiable type. A.M.*Ross*

The north end of Filey station in the mid-1950s with D49/2 No.62751 THE ALBRIGHTON awaiting departure with a Hull to Scarborough train. A number of "Hunts" and "Shires" had their original LNER group standard tenders replaced by GCR and NER types and 62751 is seen coupled to a NER tender. The water crane is of the type introduced by the NER in 1862 and has the spherical style of balance weight. According to railway staff who were employed at the station during the 1950s, when the water crane was removed it was broken into small pieces on site. This debris was then put into the drain under the site of the water crane where, presumably, it remains to this day. The roof had the hip end, seen in the photograph, removed in the late 1960s. The opposite end suffered the same fate a few years later. In 1988 British Rail proposed that the entire roof should be removed but the Minister for the Environment refused permission after considerable objections from various interested parties. Since that time, supported by a considerable financial commitment by the local authorities and English Heritage, British Rail has completed a superb job of restoring the roof to its original appearance. The result of this work is that Filey now has a unique station building as it is the only working example of a G.T.Andrews country station trainshed to retain the original roof style. J.E.F*arline collection*.

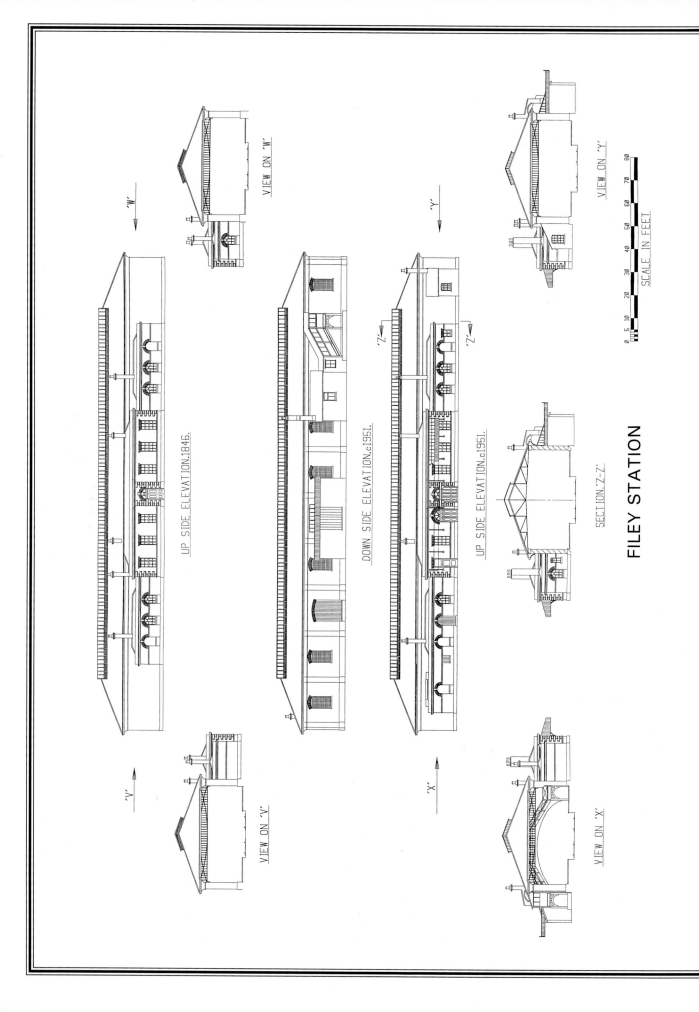

VIEW ON 'W'

VIEW ON 'Y'

VIEW ON 'V'

VIEW ON 'X'

UP SIDE ELEVATION.1846.

DOWN SIDE ELEVATION.c1951.

UP SIDE ELEVATION.c1951.

SECTION.'Z-Z'.

FILEY STATION

SCALE IN FEET

0 5 10   20   30   40   50   60   70   80

Seen here shortly after Grouping, at the south end of York station, Raven designed class Z Atlantic, 2207 gets away briskly with a Newcastle-Liverpool express. This engine would run as far as Leeds, where it would be exchanged for an LMS western division engine. On some of the cross-Pennine services this engine change took place at York, as witnessed by the presence of an ex LYR Hughes 4-6-0 outside Queen Street shed on the right. The train comprises a wonderful collection of predominantly LNWR passenger stock, but begins with a GNR bogie milk van, behind which are two LNWR 45' 0" arc roof full brakes, the leading one having already received its crimson lake livery. Behind these are an ex-works LNER luggage van and an unidentified short wheelbase vehicle. Next come five LNWR 45'0" arc roof passenger coaches, all still in LNWR livery, while a similarly painted, but more modern elliptical roof brake brings up the rear. To the left of the train the innumerable runs of point rodding, signal wires and other equipment, to operate the complex track layout, necessitates long runs of timber walkways for staff safely. W.Hudson *collection*

Even during wartime, improvements were carried out where absolutely necessary. This is the scene at York engine shed about 1943 when wet ash pits were being installed. The disruption this work must have caused would have been tremendous and would have taken the organisation of the depots working to the limits. Locomotives in view are two B16/1s and an A7 freight tank. *Authors collection.*

B1 61084, of York shed, stands with its train of vans alongside the wooden platform of Rowntrees Halt, York, in September 1950. The halt, which was opened in 1927 under the name Rowntree's Cocoa Works, was situated on a loop off the Foss Islands branch. This was 1 mile 52 chains long and left the Scarborough line a little over a mile from York station, before curving round the eastern outskirts of the city to terminate outside the city walls near Walmgate Bar. Formally opened on 8th December 1879, but not fully operational until 1st January 1880, the line gave rise to much industrial development including the gas and electricity works, Henry Leetham & Sons Ltd (Millers), various coal merchants, the NER laundry and the Derwent Valley Light Railway. Messrs Rowntree's works had its own internal rail system, connected to the branch just south of the halt, and this gave rise to a considerable amount of miscellaneous freight traffic, both in and out, well into the 1980s. The halt itself was used by both staff and parties of visitors to the factory until its closure in the 1980s. W.*Hudson collection*

(*below*) Class V2 No.60964 DURHAM LIGHT INFANTRY has steam to spare as it waits to leave York's platform 16 with a down express in about 1960. The outside platforms at York, added in 1938, present an austere contrast to those under the overall roof. The engine is one of the class which was modified with outside steam pipes in BR days. The leading coach is a Stanier open third, with a second Stanier vehicle behind, and the V2 has almost certainly just taken over a Bristol - Newcastle working. A J72 0-6-0T is standing on the middle road. Note the water crane attached to the underside of the platform awning, and the smoke deflector plates under the footbridge, both features which have long since disappeared from the railway scene.

A8 No.69881 and D49/I No.62731 SELKIRKSHIRE leave Gallows Close Yard in Scarborough with a Railway Correspondence & Travel Society railtour heading for Whitby on 23rd June 1957. Gallows Close was originally intended as the site for the southern terminus station of the Scarborough & Whitby Railway Company but this was rendered unnecessary when the NER agreed to provide accommodation at Central Station. R.J.*Buckley*

A delightful scene in August 1938 at Levisham on the now preserved Pickering to Grosmont line, as G5 0-4-4T 1886 prepares to leave with a Malton to Whitby stopping train. The station nameboard appears to be the original NER type of enamel plate, with cream letters on a chocolate background. Quite unlike the well known shade used by the GWR, the North Eastern chocolate was a warm reddish-brown colour. W.*Potter*

Grosmont Junction and station, in the mid 1950s, with the unusual design of NER signal box prominent in the centre. The box was constructed from wood and brick in a similar manner to other Southern division boxes but with the cabin overhanging the base on all four sides. In 1979 it was moved to a new site by the North York Moors Railway Trust. The main station buildings were erected adjacent to the Pickering line on the left and it is these which now form the northern terminus of the North York Moors Railway. The line to the right is the Esk Valley route to Middlesborough. Note the very long check rails required on the tight curve. In the right background is a water tower with an adjacent water crane of typical NER design. *R.J.Buckley.*

Battersby, on the Esk valley line, was one of those isolated rural stations opened simply because there was a junction. Beyond the signal box was Battersby North Junction, where the line to Middlesbrough branched left from the line to Whitby. At the opposite end of the station was Battersby South Junction where the mineral railway to Rosedale branched in a generally southerly direction from the line to Picton, on the ECML. The former route closed entirely in 1928, while that to Picton lost its passenger services in June 1954. In this view, from the station footbridge, in the mid 1950s, the 7.57 a.m. to Whitby sets off in a cloud of steam, while the 6.49 a.m. Whitby to Middlesbrough train stands at the adjacent platform. The train engine is standing somewhere behind the cameraman waiting to complete its run-round movement once the Whitby train has gone. The driver of this engine has been very quick off the mark, as has the guard in changing the tail lamp, for if running to time the Middlesborough train has only been at the platform two minutes. *R.J.Buckley*

B1 61038 BLACKTAIL drifts through Sleights station with the 2.10 p.m. stopping train from Whitby Town to Leeds. Situated in the beautiful valley of the River Esk, which runs just behind the trees on the left, Sleights is approximately mid-way between Whitby and Grosmont. Seen here from the Pickering - Whitby road, the view is full of interesting details, particularly to the modeller. In the background is the small, brick-built NER signal box, close to which is a pedestrian girder bridge over the river. Just in front of this is the yard weigh office which is tilted precariously towards the river. The GNR six wheel non-corridor third in the foreground is being used as a tool van by the Permanent Way department, who also have use of the low sided wagon with its group of cans and drums. The primitive coal staithes, built from sacks of coal are of interest, but even more so are the full sacks of coal in the adjacent open wagon. There are also empty sacks draped over the wagon sides, and some by the coal on the ground. As far as the authors are aware pre-bagged coal was never carried from the colliery by rail. One possibility is that the coal has been acquired from another merchant who had excess stocks, or it could be going out under similar circumstances. More likely it was being delivered to signal boxes and stations along the line. A.M.*Ross*

Class A8 No.9881, leaves the south end of the Esk viaduct with a Whitby - Scarborough stopping train of non-corridor stock which comprises two ex NER vehicles, followed by an LNER built Gresley third, and a GNR brake third. The Esk viaduct was the major engineering feature of the Scarborough to Whitby line and was 915 feet long, with a height from river bed to parapet of 125 feet. The average span of the thirteen arches was 60 feet, with the central one over the river being 64 feet. Work on the viaduct began on 17th October 1882 and was completed in October 1884, at an approximate cost of £40,000. The first train to use the structure passed over on the 24th of

that month. It is fortuitous that the well known Whitby photographer, Frank M. Sutcliffe, was active at that time and there exists today an invaluable photographic record of the construction of the viaduct. The locomotive in this view became a 'film star' just after World War II, when it was used to haul a train in the feature film *Holiday Camp*. The film was made on location at Butlin's camp, Filey, but it was decided that the newly built Camp station was not sufficiently attractive. The station seen in the film was that at Sandsend, just north of Whitby, and number 9881 was specially cleaned up for its starring role in the opening scenes.

23rd June 1957 and the RCTS tour again. 69881, which had earlier double-headed 62731 SELKIRKSHIRE from Scarborough, has run round the train at Whitby West Cliff Station. The tank engine is now at the head of the train for the reversal down to Prospect Hill Junction and then on to Whitby Town. Note the signalling of the station for bi-directional operation. The line straight ahead (just look at that gradient) is to Middlesborough via Redcar along the coast. A variation on the standard NER cast iron footbridge connects the platforms. R.J.*Buckley*.

Whitby Town Station was built by George Hudson's York & North Midland Railway which had purchased the Whitby & Pickering Railway in June 1845. The station was, of course, designed by the Y&NMR's architect George Townsend Andrews of York. At the time of this mid 1950s photograph the train shed had lost its overall roof which was typical of so many of Andrew's station designs. Class A8 4-6-2T 69854 awaits its departure with the 5.35 p.m. stopping train to Battersby. On the left, B.R. Standard class 4MT 2-6-4T 80119 prepares to leave with the 4.20 p.m. to Scarborough. R.J.*Buckley*.

The bleakness of the northern section of the Yorkshire coastal route is captured in this view as class G5, No.7349 crosses the viaduct over Newholm Beck, between Sandsend and Whitby, with a southbound stopping train. In the background stands the headland of Sandsend Ness, while to the left can be seen the Whitby to Sandsend road. The tubular iron viaduct is one of five similar structures built to carry the line over the valleys which ran down to the sea between Redcar and Whitby. The train of ex NER non-corridor stock consists of brake third, composite, brake third, and apart from the locomotive livery the whole scene could be in pre-grouping days, although it was captured in 1947. W.Hudson *collection*

With the North Sea in the background, A8 class 9881, hauls a northbound stopping train along the cliff side above what is thought to be Sandsend, on a sunny afternoon in the late 1940s. The train consists of an ex NER 10 ton fish van, a Gresley non-corridor brake third and four ex NER non-corridor coaches. The A8's were regular performers on the sinuous, hilly coast line between Scarborough and Whitby, the former being the home of 9881 for many years before withdrawal in June 1958. W.Hudson *collection*

The Whitby to Middlesbrough coastal line was almost as desolate as routes traversing the Pennines and is typified here in this view of Kettleness station, on 18th April 1958. Construction of the line was begun by the Whitby, Redcar & Middlesbrough Railway, but the company was soon in difficulties and the NER was asked to take over, which it did under an Act of Parliament of 19th July 1875. In this view class J25 0-6-0 No.65648, complete with buffer beam snowplough, slows down to enable the single line token to be taken. The engine is returning to Whitby after working the three times a week Whitby to Crag Hall pick-up goods. The neat and tidy appearance of the station, with its platform mounted signal box, belies the fact that it had less than a month to survive, for it was closed entirely on 5th May 1958.   A.M.Ross

As it followed the coast it was only natural that the Middlesborough to Whitby line should encounter many valleys, five of which were deep enough to require viaducts. Of these the largest was Staithes viaduct, 152 ft high above the Roxby Beck. It had six 60 ft long spans and eleven 30 ft long. Although completed four years before the Tay Bridge disaster of December 1879, the viaduct had not been brought into use and as a consequence of the Scottish tragedy, extensive cross-bracing was added. It also carried a wind gauge and whenever wind pressure reached 28 lb per sq.ft it caused a bell to ring in Staithes signal box. All traffic was then stopped until the wind eased. In this circa 1957 view, one of Thompson's class L1 2-6-4Ts, No.67754, travels south towards Whitby with a stopping passenger train, composed of a Thompson non-corridor brake composite, three ex NER non-corridor thirds and a Thompson brake third.

Before World War Two, Harrogate enjoyed a comprehensive train service over the seven routes radiating from the town. These included long distance services such as Liverpool - Newcastle, and the prestige Pullman services to the capital. Local services ran to Leeds, Bradford, Pateley Bridge, Ripon, Pilmoor, York and Church Fenton. By the mid 1950s however, closures and rationalisation had bitten deeply and local services were primarily those to Leeds and York. In this view N1 0-6-2T 69484 stands at the northbound main line platform at Harrogate with a train from Leeds Central. These engines were rare visitors to the town and as far as the authors are aware the first recorded working of an N1 to Harrogate was during the 1955 ASLEF strike, when a skeleton service was operated by NUR union members. However very careful scrutiny of the original photograph shows the shed plate to be 56B, the number allocated to Ardsley following the regional boundary changes at the end of 1956. Thus the view falls between January 1957 and early 1959, when 69484 was withdrawn. At this time LNER, and pre-group coaching stock, was still much in evidence, but it was showing its age. The Gresley 6-compartment brake third, seen behind the engine, has had the side sheeting of the two compartments next to the brake end repaired by a metal plate, a common practice at the time. Also worthy of note to the modeller is the support post and bracing wires to the water column, which spans two tracks. N.E.*Stead.*

Seen here in 1959 the concourse to platform 5 is full of nostalgic atmosphere and detail, prominent among which is the ironwork carrying the roof. In the foreground the circulating area has a minimum number of columns and the larger spans necessitate deep H-section girders, carried on slender columns, with fluted tops and simple, yet elegant cast iron brackets. From the main girder, lightweight transverse girders, each as a series of circles, run out to support the platform awning. These girders are again supported on lightweight columns, without fluted tops, but a more substantial twin bracket. Below this ironwork the station was always well kept and during the 1920s and 30s it was well known for its floral displays, entirely in keeping with the environment of the town as a whole. An added factor in this caring attitude was that the station was frequented by members of the royal family travelling to and from Harewood House, a few miles to the south of the town. Other details worthy of note include the cast iron platform fencing and the neat, wooden, ticket collectors office, the pillar box with two stamp issuing machines attached and the line of posters proclaiming the delights of York, Whitley Bay, Deal, Thornton Clevelys, Portsmouth & Southsea and Clacton-on-Sea. Almost lost in this sea of detail is the class J39 0-6-0 passing through on the down through road with an ex-NER clerestory roof coach, which is probably an engineers inspection saloon. Finally one might wonder, over 30 years on, if John Farrah is still making his Harrogate Toffee. W.*Hudson collection*

The first station in Harrogate was known as Brunswick and was opened in July 1848 as the terminus of the York & North Midland branch from Church Fenton and Wetherby. However passenger traffic on this branch was never significant for Harrogate's affinities lay with Leeds. Connections between the two came a little nearer some twelve months later when the Leeds & Thirsk Railway opened, but this line was barred from entry to Harrogate by Almscliff bank and followed the much easier route through the Crimple valley to Starbeck. Following the formation of the NER in 1854 the matter was looked at again and in August 1859 an Act was obtained sanctioning, inter alia, a new centrally situated station and a link from just north of Pannal, on the L&T line, to a point south of Crimple viaduct on the Y&NM branch. This link and the new station were opened on 1st August 1862, together with a northern link which took through trains back on to the L&T at Bilton Road Junction. Harrogate, now very much a resort and dormitory town for Leeds, Bradford and York, owes its existence to the mineral springs discovered around the end of the sixteenth century. By the mid Nineteenth century it had become highly fashionable among the more wealthy sections of society to 'take the waters' and this must have been at the forefront of Thomas Prosser's mind when he designed what must be accepted as a quite lavish station for a town the size of Harrogate. What is puzzling is why it was felt necessary to provide quadruple tracks through the station when virtually every passenger train stopped there and most freight traffic was routed via Starbeck. The size of the station can be gauged from this view in March 1959 looking south from platform 4 across to No.5, and the bay platforms 6 and 7. Of particular note is the double-sided catch point on the down through road. In the event of a runaway, this would allow the signalman to assess the position of any passenger trains standing in the station, and then divert the offending vehicles accordingly. Having said that there must have been compelling reasons for installing the catch points within station limits in the first place. Another unusual feature is the home signal for the down through road which is mounted on a horizontal bar extending out from the platform building and guyed to the platform canopy. A little to the right is another unusual signal, this time underslung from a vertical post attached to the canopy ironworks. As one would have expected platform 5 to be the main up platform the siting of this signal can only be a very early example of today's common signalling for bi-directional running. W.*Hudson collection*

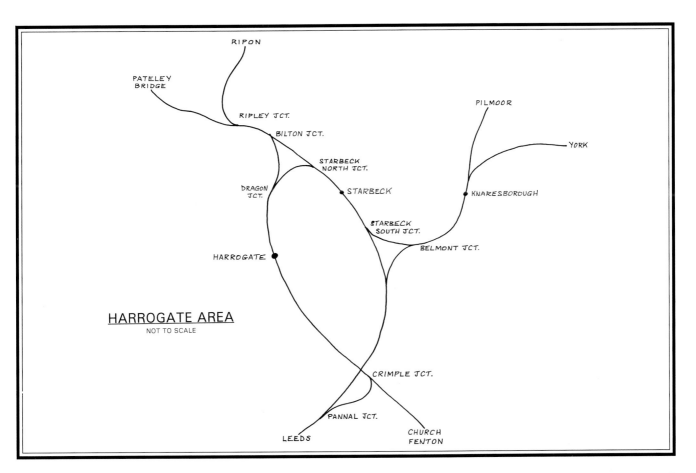

HARROGATE AREA
NOT TO SCALE

Edward Thompson's rebuild of Gresley's class D49 4-4-0, No.62768, THE MORPETH, and its crew, pose for the camera at Harrogate station about 1950. As LNER 365, the engine was modified in 1942 from a 3-cylinder engine to one with two inside cylinders, these being the same design as those fitted to the GCR 'Directors'. The engine was given the class designation D under Thompson's standardisation plan for the LNER. The modifications resulted in a reduction of tractive effort from 21,556 lbs to 19,890 lbs and a reduction in weight of 2½ tons. Unfortunately, as with Thompson's redesign of other Gresley locomotives, the modified form did not perform as well as the original. It ended its life at Starbeck shed in October 1952 after being involved in a collision during a shunting movement. The front end of the engine was so severely damaged that Darlington Works decided to cut up the engine. W.Hudson *collection*.

A3 60036 COLOMBO passes Dragon junction, just north of Harrogate, with a southbound Newcastle to Liverpool express. The train is running on the line from Northallerton. To the right, behind the signalbox, is the line to Starbeck, Knaresborough and York. Note the substantial cottages on the right which were built for the use of railway employees. J.W.*Armstrong*

Most local trains between Leeds and Harrogate followed the old Leeds Northern line via Bramhope tunnel and Arthington, but until its closure in 1964 a few trains followed the hilly route through Crossgates and Wetherby. For most of the post-war years these trains were in the hands of Starbeck's stud of 'Hunt' class D49/2 4-4-0s, as typified by this view of 62765 THE GOATHLAND, with a Leeds bound service at Wetherby, in the mid 1950s. The train is made up of a neat set of NER five compartment brake third, lavatory composite and a second brake third. The lines converging on Wetherby, from Leeds, Harrogate and Church Fenton were all closed to passenger traffic on 6th January 1964, but as late as the early 1960s the Leeds-Wetherby route was graced by regular Liverpool - Newcastle expresses, which served Harrogate without the need to reverse at Leeds City. W.A.*Camwell*

Class G5 0-4-4T 67253 stands at the picturesque station of Dacre with a down train on the Ripley Junction to Pateley Bridge branch. The branch was opened in 1862, at which time Thomas Prosser was the company architect. Perhaps most widely known for his major works, such as York, he also introduced a simple, rustic design for country stations, featuring bold crow step gables. In addition to the Pateley Bridge branch, this design was found on the Esk Valley line and the Lanchester Valley, in County Durham. 67253 worked the branch for almost 33 years, being fitted with push-pull apparatus in 1939. After withdrawal of passenger services on 2nd April 1951 the engine was transferred to the East Riding and was withdrawn from Hull Botanic Gardens in 1958/59. B.G.*Tweed*.

The terminus of the branch was at Pateley Bridge, some 14½ miles from Harrogate, seen here about 1950, with the single coach branch passenger train, which made four or five return journeys daily. The locomotive, class G5, No.67284, of Starbeck shed, still carries the early livery of BRITISH RAILWAYS, applied up to the adoption of the lion-over-wheel totem in 1949, but the 6-compartment brake third still carries its NER number 2418. The G5 met an earlier fate than its sister engine in the previous plate, being withdrawn from Darlington toward the end of 1956. Rail transport continued a further 6 miles up the valley in the shape of the Nidd Valley Light Railway, opened on 11th September 1907, from its own station in Pateley Bridge to Lofthouse-in-Nidderdale. Opened to facilitate the construction of reservoirs by Bradford Corporation, this line carried a limited passenger service, but was closed entirely on 1st January 1930, when it was no longer required for the carriage of men and building materials. W.A.*Camwell*

D49/2 No.62755 THE BILSDALE, of Starbeck shed, heads north past Wormald Green signal box, south of Ripon, with a down express about 1955. The station buildings can just be seen on the left, while the trailing turnout in the left foreground gave access to the goods yard. The slotted post signal seen above the engine is the Down starter, sited to protect the level crossing. The one above the third coach is the inner home, the two combining to give a very short section, virtually no longer than the station platforms. The leading coach is a North Eastern corridor brake third, while the remainder of the train comprises a mixture of Gresley and Thompson vehicles. *J.Bateman collection*

B16/1 No.61428 sets off from Ripon with a northbound relief train from Leeds in the mid 1950s. Above the fourth coach can just be seen a rather unusual water crane which was attached to the platform awning and had a pulley system to enable it to be swung out as required. Ripon was the terminus for trains on the Masham branch, but the most frequent service was that provided by the Leeds - Northallerton trains. However judging by the length of the train seen here, it is a longer distance working and may well be a Leeds to Newcastle relief. The leading coach in the train is a Gresley GNR brake composite, behind which is a Gresley corridor composite, then a Thompson corridor first, followed by a Gresley corridor third. Behind these are three more Thompson and two Gresley coaches. Like that at Wormald Green, the signal box is a standard NER type S4 box, introduced in 1905. *J.E.Farline collection*

J39/1 0-6-0 No.64861, of Starbeck shed, comes off the Masham branch with a through freight train. Although one would expect the train to be running under class K headlamps (pick-up or branch freight), no doubt by the time it had taken up stock at Ripon and stations to Harrogate it would indeed be a through freight train. While the leading low sided wagon must have carried a special load, the covered van for merchandise and the 16 ton all-steel mineral wagon for coal were all that would be required for a two station branch line as BR lost interest in pick-up freight traffic in the late 1950s/early 1960s. The train is running down the rear of the main line platform at Melmerby, where the double sided nameboard would remind passengers that they were approaching the branch platform. The passenger service to Masham was withdrawn as early as 1st January 1931, but goods traffic lingered on until the line was closed completely on 11th November 1963. J.Bateman *collection*

J25 65693 leaves the yard at Thirsk with a down train of empties in 1951. The second wagon of its train is a pre-1923 12 ton private owner, still fitted with grease axleboxes, and carrying the remnants of Firbeck colliery livery. The lines curving away to the right go to Melmerby and the junction with the line from Northallerton to Ripon and Harrogate. The line to Melmerby was closed in 1959. In 1905 the NER brought into use, between Thirsk and Alne, a number of American-style automatic semaphore signals, which were installed by the Hall Automatic Signal Co. of New York. These signals, which were operated by compressed carbon dioxide gas stored in cylinders at the base of each post, gave good service until they were replaced by colour light signals in 1933. The latter can be seen, on the main line, just behind the second and fourth wagons. Note the standard NER cast iron panel water tank on top of a stone base. In the right background is the closed engine shed which had housed its last engines (a pair of J25's) in November 1930; still intact and complete with doors in this view, the shed was finally demolished in 1965. 65693 remained in the Northallerton area until it was transferred to Hull (Dairycoates) in January 1957, from where it was withdrawn in April 1962. *Locofotos.*

An engine from Colwick shed (38A) is a long way from home as it heads northwards through Thirsk station on the East Coast main line in the mid 1950s with a varied collection of mineral wagons in tow. The locomotive is class K2/2 2-6-0 No.61753 and displays its home depot on the LMS/BR-type smokebox door shedplate and also, LNER style, on the buffer beam. J.E.*Farline collection.*

Its early 1950s and G5 0-4-4T 67289 awaits departure time at Boroughbridge on the branch line from Knaresborough to Pilmoor on the East Coast main line. This line was built as two separate branches. Pilmoor to Boroughbridge was opened on 17th June 1847 and Knaresborough to Boroughbridge on 1st April 1875. Note that the station nameboard reads "Borough Bridge", and appears to have been painted by hand so it is probably a mistake by the signwriter. Although the engine has received its BR number it still sports the legend LNER on its tanks and has yet to be fitted with a smokebox numberplate. The train comprises a typical branch line set of brake third/composite/brake third. W.A.*Camwell.*

A3 60073 ST GATIEN roars through Pilmoor station with the up 'Tees-Tyne Pullman', on one of those rare occasions when a named train ran without its customary headboard. The rather austere footbridge was erected at the time of widening, as was the new down plat-form, on the left. The station building follows the same architectural style as the signal box, while the concrete post and tube fencing contrasts sharply with the NER fencing on the up platform. J.F.*Sedgwick*

Class D20 4-4-0 No.62388 stands alongside the platform-mounted signal box at Jervaulx station on the Northallerton to Hawes Junction line in June 1957. The station building has the typical stepped gables found at other locations on North Riding branch lines. However, this was not a standard feature on the Wensleydale branch, for the line was built in three stages and different architectural styles were used. As was often the case the shelter on the opposite platform is a simple wooden structure and the platform is built up using six layers of interlaced sleepers, with an ash or ballast infilling. On top of this is a row of equally spaced cross members, at 90 degrees to the track, above which is a decking again from sleepers. Careful study of the original photograph suggests that this is covered by a bitumen sheet topped with a layer of gravel chippings. The pile of sleepers on the platform which, judging by the weeds growing round them, have been there for some time and would cause apoplexy to today's Health and Safety inspectors. J.W.*Armstrong*

G5 0-4-4T 7309 about to depart from Richmond with a stopping train to Darlington. The station, designed by G.T.Andrews, was built on the opposite side of the River Swale to the town and included in the construction work was a bridge to give access for passengers from the town. To make it more compatible with the local architecture the station building was designed in a gothic style although the other railway buildings, i.e. engine shed, goods warehouse, etc, were to standard designs used elsewhere. Note the very basic method used to block off the line on the left. The pointwork is supported by interlaced sleepers; a typical NER feature. The second coach of the train is a Gresley semi-corridor lavatory composite but the others are all ex-NER. W.A.*Camwell.*

G5 0-4-4T 67273 stands with its train at the single platform at Middleton-In-Teesdale in the mid 1950s. This station was the terminus of a branch line from Barnard Castle in County Durham which was opened on 12th May 1868. Although Middleton-In-Teesdale was in County Durham, the station was built on the opposite bank of the River Tees and was, therefore, in the North Riding of Yorkshire. The station building seen in the photograph replaced the original in 1888/9. On the right is the single road engine shed. This was a sub-shed of Darlington and was in use up to the introduction of diesel multiple units on 16th September 1957. A 45ft diameter turntable was situated just beyond the water tank but by the date of the photograph it had been filled in. Behind the engine is the goods warehouse and beyond that the elevator housing for a tarmacadam plant which had its own private siding. J.W.*Armstrong.*